WTF

I Did Not Sign Up For This!

A Guide to Not Just Surviving, but
Thriving in Menopause and
Beyond

Tina Lund Pehrsson

TABLE OF CONTENTS

INTRODUCTION

When I had my first hot flash, I was honestly impressed and surprised. I called my mom to share my excitement over this experience. I was amazed at how much heat the body can actually produce from the center just sitting still. She laughed and said, "Hold on to that thought, honey; next time, you might not find it that great."

And she was right! It sucks! Even if I'm one of the lucky ones who doesn't seem to get many, they always seem to excel in bad timing. Like in the middle of a meeting.

Some women celebrate their menopause as a milestone of freedom and wisdom, while others mourn the loss of their fertility and youth. Either way, it's a good excuse to throw a party and have some cake.

This is meant to be used as you like; read it all in one go, or find the chapters when you need them. I´ve included blank pages after each chapter for you to write down your thoughts, what you tried, and, most importantly, what worked. Nobody can say for sure what will give you relief. We are all deliciously different.

I do not claim to be an expert, but rather a nurse by profession, drawing on my own journey, the extensive research I did online and through books, and the invaluable guidance I´ve received along the way.

Even the most composed individuals encounter moments of vulnerability, such as the universally relatable experience of hot flashes. Even cool people can get to hot.

Within these pages, I aim to offer guidance, support, and reassurance in the challenges you may face.

Chapter 1
Understanding Menopause

What is Menopause?

Menopause is a natural biological process that marks the end of a woman's reproductive years. It typically occurs between the ages of 45 and 55. Menopause is defined as the absence of menstrual periods for 12 consecutive months, indicating that the ovaries have ceased to release eggs and produce hormones such as estrogen and progesterone. So, on the positive side, no more cramps, no more bloodstains and no more worrying about getting pregnant.

During menopause, we experience various physical and emotional changes due to the fluctuation and drop in hormone levels.

These changes can have a significant impact on our overall well-being and quality of life.

Understanding the different aspects of menopause is helpful in going through this transitional phase.

Menopause and Sexual Health

Hormonal changes during menopause can also impact your sexual health. Reduced estrogen levels can cause vaginal dryness, decreased libido, and discomfort during intercourse. Open communication with your partner and healthcare provider is crucial to address these issues and explore available treatment options. It really doesn't have to be the end of your sex life.

With the right help and patience, it can get even better than ever.

Open communication with a partner and exploring different lubricants or hormone replacement therapy options can help maintain a satisfying sex life. Be kind to yourself always.

Menopause and Mental Health

One common concern during menopause is the impact on mental health. Hormone fluctuations can disrupt neurotransmitters in the brain, causing these emotional changes.

Many women experience symptoms such as mood swings, irritability, anxiety, and even depression.

These changes are primarily attributed to the hormonal imbalances occurring in the body.

It may help you to seek support and engage in self-care practices to manage your mental health during this time.

Treat yourself as an old friend; be kind and patient.

Menopause and Sleep Issues

Many experience sleep disturbances during menopause, including insomnia, night sweats, and hot flashes.

Lack of sleep can affect overall health and well-being. Implementing good sleep hygiene practices, such as establishing a regular sleep schedule and creating a relaxing bedtime routine, can help improve sleep quality.

Menopause and Exercise

Regular exercise is highly beneficial during menopause. It helps improve mood and overall mental well-being, helps manage weight gain, reduces the risk of chronic diseases like heart disease and osteoporosis. Menopause can impact your exercise routine. Hormonal changes may cause a decrease in bone density, muscle mass, and metabolism.

However, regular physical activity can help counteract these effects, improve overall health, and manage menopausal symptoms.

Engaging in weight-bearing exercises, strength training, and cardiovascular activities can enhance bone health, maintain muscle tone, and boost energy levels.

However, menopause can bring about changes in energy levels and joint health, making it essential to adapt exercise routines accordingly.

Engaging in low-impact exercises like swimming, cycling, or yoga can help manage weight, reduce bone loss, and improve overall mental well-being.

If you have never really done any exercise, it will take a bigger effort, but you are doing it for you.

Just you showing yourself some love. Even if it doesn't feel like it in the beginning.

Navigating menopause can be challenging, but understanding its different aspects can empower you to make informed decisions about your health and well-being. Menopause is a unique journey for all of us, but it can be helpful to understand the different stages that we commonly go through during this transitional phase. Knowledge gives you the power to choose what you want to do or not do.

I just want to help you see some options, so you can make informed choices fit for your life.

Pelvic Floor Exercises: This is important! Peeing your pants while sneezing is no fun. Peeing your pants laughing is better, but still not really what anyone wants, right? Menopause can lead to a weakening of the pelvic floor muscles, resulting in urinary incontinence and reduced sexual satisfaction. Pelvic floor exercises, such as Kegels, help strengthen these muscles, enhance bladder control, and improve sexual health.

I use The Empelvic pillow, and it really worked wonders for me.

Perimenopause is the first stage of menopause and can start as early as 30s or 40s.

During this time, hormone levels fluctuate, leading to irregular menstrual cycles and various physical and emotional symptoms. Hot flashes, night sweats, mood swings, and sleep disturbances are common occurrences during perimenopause.

This stage can last for several years before menopause officially begins.

It is the warm up face, the "get ready! here we go."

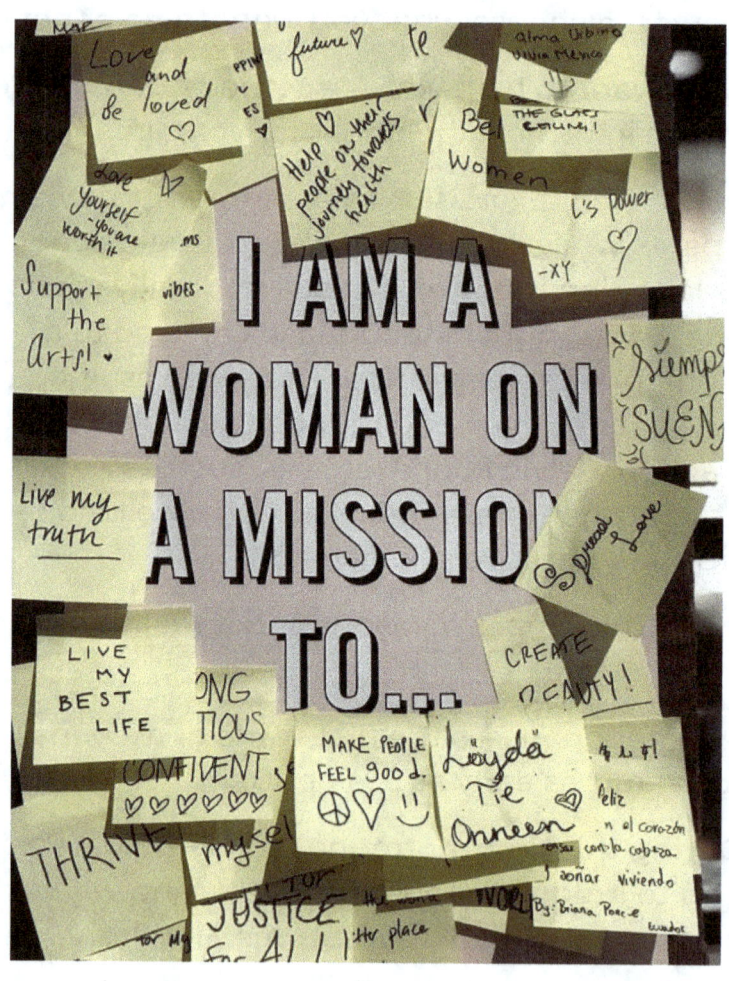

Postmenopause is the stage that follows menopause and lasts for the remainder of our lives. During this time, symptoms associated with menopause may continue, but they generally become less frequent and severe. However, it is crucial to remember that postmenopausal women are still at risk for certain health conditions, such as osteoporosis and heart disease, due to the decrease in estrogen levels.

Regular health check-ups and lifestyle adjustments are important during this stage.

My notes

CHAPTER 2
SEXUAL HEALTH

Changes in Libido and Desire

One of the most common and significant changes women experience during menopause is a shift in our libido and desire.

The decline in hormone production, specifically estrogen and progesterone, can lead to changes in libido and desire.

You are not a dried-out old hag; you are changing.

Getting in the mood and getting the body ready may take longer, but you are also more experienced.

So, take advantage of your knowledge, take your time, and show yourself some patience and respect.

This decline in libido can be attributed to various factors, including hormonal changes, physical discomfort, and emotional stress.

It is essential to remember that every woman's experience is unique, and some may not experience a significant shift in their sexual desire.

If you are that lucky, ENJOY!!

Menopause can also affect mental health, which in turn can impact sexual desire.

Mood swings, anxiety, and depression are common symptoms during this phase of life. These mental health challenges can influence a woman's interest in intimacy and create additional barriers to sexual satisfaction.

More about that in chapter 9, Mental health

Furthermore, menopause can bring about sleep issues, such as insomnia or night sweats.

Lack of quality sleep can lead to fatigue and decreased energy levels, which can further reduce sexual desire.

It is crucial to address these sleep disturbances through various strategies like creating a sleep-friendly environment and establishing a consistent bedtime routine.

More about this topic in chapter 3, Sleep Issues

Engaging in physical activity can positively impact sexual health.

Exercise increases blood flow to the genital area, enhances body confidence, and promotes overall well-being, which can contribute to a healthier libido and desire.

More about this is in chapter 4, Exercise

Dealing with libido changes during menopause is like navigating a rollercoaster ride with your partner (if you have one) and healthcare provider as your trusty co-pilots!

Chatting openly, getting your partner´s support, and trying out fun intimacy tricks can keep your sexual spark alive.

Plus, there are plenty of remedies like hormone replacement, natural remedies, or funky lubricants to ease any discomfort.

More about this in chapter 5, Managing symptoms naturally and chapter 6, Hormonal Replacement Therapy

Don´t forget to share with your friends if you find a cool gynecologist who´s a menopause expert!

Menopause might throw some curveballs at your libido, but remember, every woman´s journey is like her own unique dance floor.

You can totally rock your way through menopause and still have a blast in the bedroom.

Some women find that lubricants, supplements, or toys can enhance their sexual pleasure.

Others find that romance, intimacy, or humor can spice up their sex life.

Whatever works for you, just remember that you're still sexy, and you deserve to have fun.

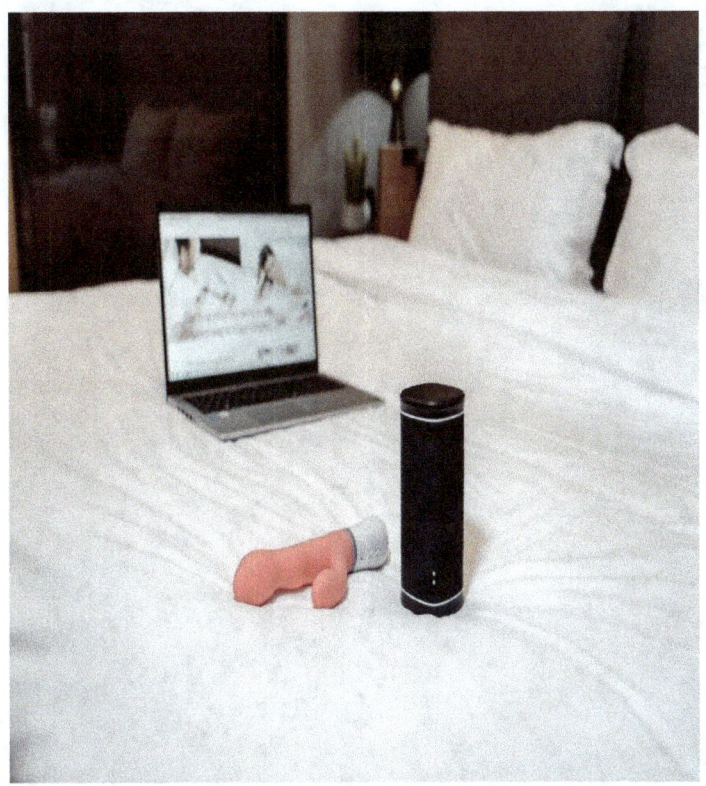

Aloe Vera: Aloe Vera gel, known for its soothing properties, can provide relief from vaginal dryness when applied externally. Make sure to use pure aloe vera gel without added chemicals or fragrances.

Soy Products: Soy contains phytoestrogens, plant-based compounds that mimic estrogen in the body. Incorporating soy products like tofu, soy milk, or edamame into your diet may help alleviate vaginal dryness in some women.

Let's talk about Vaginal Dryness

One of the most common and frustrating symptoms experienced by women in menopause is vaginal dryness, which can lead to painful intercourse. Along with the cessation of periods, menopause brings about various changes in the body, including vaginal dryness. This occurs as estrogen levels decrease, leading to thinning and drying of the vaginal tissues. As a result, many women experience discomfort, pain, and even bleeding during sexual intercourse.

Understanding the impact of vaginal dryness on sexual health is crucial. It can hinder intimacy, strain relationships, and negatively affect your self-esteem and mental well-being.

There are several effective treatments available for managing vaginal dryness and painful intercourse during menopause. One option is hormone replacement therapy (HRT), which helps replenish estrogen levels and restore moisture to the vaginal tissues. However, it is crucial to consult a healthcare professional to determine if HRT is suitable for you, as it may not be recommended for everyone. More about HRT in chapter 7

Other options that might be helpful are:

Stay hydrated: Drinking plenty of water helps maintain overall hydration levels in the body, including the vaginal tissues. Adequate hydration can contribute to maintaining natural lubrication.

Healthy fats in diet: Consuming foods rich in omega-3 fatty acids, such as salmon, flaxseeds, and walnuts, can help support the body's production of lubricating oils.

Regular exercise: during menopause can have a positive impact on both physical and emotional well-being. Engaging in activities that you enjoy, such as walking, swimming, dancing or yoga, can help reduce stress, improve mood, and promote better sleep. Exercise also releases endorphins, which are known as "feel-good" hormones, providing a natural mood boost. (chapter 4 - get inspired)

Vaginal moisturizers: Natural oils such as coconut oil, olive oil or vitamin E oil can be applied to the vaginal area to help moisturize dry tissues. However, it's important to use these oils with caution, as they may degrade latex condoms and increase the risk of breakage.

Herbal Supplements: Certain herbs like black cohosh, dong quai and red clover have estrogenic properties and are believed to help balance hormone levels, potentially improving vaginal moisture. However, it's essential to consult with a healthcare provider before taking any herbal supplements, especially if you have underlying medical conditions or are taking medications.

<u>Empelvic pillow and Kegel Exercises:</u>
Strengthening the pelvic floor muscles is important and, with the right instruction, not difficult.

The Empelvic pillow and the exercises that come with it are very efficient. Easy to use and can improve vaginal tone and elasticity, which may help alleviate symptoms of dryness.

Kegel exercises are very useful as well and easy to find. Go to YouTube, find a video and try it out.

Regular sexual activity: Sexual arousal and activity can increase blood flow to the vaginal tissues, promoting natural lubrication. Regular sexual activity, with adequate foreplay and lubrication, can help prevent and alleviate vaginal dryness. Sex with a partner or masturbating both works.

Avoid irritants: Certain products like scented soaps, douches and perfumed hygiene products can disrupt the natural pH balance of the vagina and contribute to dryness. Opt for gentle, fragrance–free products to cleanse the vaginal area.

Communicate openly with your partner about these changes; you might want to reassure them that it is not a reflection of their desirability. Discuss possible solutions together, such as using lubricants or exploring alternative intimate activities. Open dialogue can help maintain a healthy sexual connection.

My notes

Chapter 3
Sleep Issues

Understanding Sleep Changes During Menopause

Sleep is an essential aspect of our overall well-being, affecting various aspects of our physical and mental health. As we navigate the menopause journey, we often experience significant changes in our sleep patterns. The decrease in estrogen levels during menopause can contribute to insomnia, making it harder to fall asleep or stay asleep.

First and foremost, it is a great help to establish a consistent sleep schedule:

Going to bed and waking up at the same time every day, even on weekends, helps regulate the body's internal clock. This consistency trains the brain to recognize when it's time to sleep, making it easier to fall asleep and stay asleep throughout the night. It might sound boring, but it can really make a difference and give you the energy to enjoy life.

Creating a relaxing bedtime routine is also beneficial: Engaging in activities that promote relaxation, such as taking a warm bath, practicing deep breathing exercises, or reading a book, can signal to the body that it's time to wind down.

Make sure your bedroom is sleep-friendly: Dim the light or make it all dark, cool and quiet. Consider using blackout curtains or an eye mask to block out any unwanted light. If noise is an issue, use earplugs or white noise to create a peaceful ambiance.

Choosing breathable bedding materials like cotton can help regulate body temperature.

Some find relief by using cooling pillows and blankets. My husband suffers from night sweats and it helped him tremendously.

Keeping a glass of cold water nearby to sip on if you wake up feeling hot can help, too.

Keeping the bedroom cool and using a fan can also alleviate discomfort. Sleep with an open window, turn up the air conditioning.

Use the options you have

I'm one of the crazy people who enjoy ice bathing, and I found that my body has become better at regulating temperature. My hands and feet no longer get as freezing during the day and I don't have night sweats. Mainly, I just like the feeling and yes, it does make me feel like a bad a**. But most of all, it improves my mood and I actually sleep better when I get my cold plunge regularly. So, if you feel like it, check it out.

Just turning the shower to cold for a minute or two in the morning, if nothing else it forces you to be present in that moment.

Whatever works for you, just remember that you're not a vampire, and you need some rest.

Exploring Sleep Aids and Medications
When experiencing sleep issues related to menopause, it may be helpful to consult a healthcare professional. They can provide guidance on hormone therapy or other medications that can alleviate symptoms and improve sleep quality.

Additionally, cognitive-behavioral therapy for insomnia (CBT-I) has been proven effective in helping women manage sleep disturbances during menopause.

Some find relief from over-the-counter sleep aids, such as melatonin or herbal supplements like valerian root and chamomile. These natural remedies can help regulate sleep patterns and promote relaxation. However, it's important to note that their effectiveness may vary from person to person, so you might need to try different options to find what works best for you.

In cases where sleep issues are more severe, prescription medications may be recommended. These include sedatives, antidepressants, and anti-anxiety medications. These medications can help improve sleep quality and reduce symptoms of anxiety and depression that often accompany menopause.

My husband had cancer and at that time, all bets were off; sleep routines were almost impossible to keep up and all my other usual go-to options weren't enough. So, my doctor gave me a prescription for motion sickness medicine that also makes you sleepy. That was exactly what I needed to get my head above water again. Please seek help when you need it.

However, it's crucial to consult with a healthcare professional before starting any prescription medication, as they may have potential risks and interactions with other medications.

My notes

_____

_____

_____

_____

_____

_____

_____

_____

_____

_____

_____

_____

_____

_____

_____

_____

_____

_____

_____

_____

_____

_____

Chapter 4
Exercise

The Importance of Exercise During Menopause

Let's be honest, like it or not we all benefit from getting exercise. It doesn't have to be complicated or time-consuming. Every time you get your butt off the couch counts.

Coffee dates with friends can be walk and talk too. And sometimes working harder, not smarter, is the smart thing to do. Find ways to get steps in, take the stairs and do things standing instead of sitting. And remember to celebrate every time you do. Give yourself a high five if no one is around to give you one.

One of the most significant benefits of exercise during menopause is its positive impact on menopause-related mental health issues. Hormonal fluctuations during this time can lead to mood swings, anxiety, and depression. Engaging in physical activity releases endorphins, which are chemicals in the brain that promote feelings of happiness and reduce stress.

Regular exercise can help stabilize your mood, improve your mental well-being, and boost your self-esteem.

You might even get addicted in the best way.

I love my workouts.

I know I might sound nuts, but exercising makes me feel happy, proud of myself and, as a bonus, more attractive and more in the mood for intimacy.

Many experience hot flashes and night sweats, which can disturb our sleep and cause frequent awakenings throughout the night.

These interruptions can lead to feelings of fatigue, irritability, and difficulty concentrating during the day.

Yes, the drop in estrogen is just the gift that keeps on giving. But understanding might help lessen the frustration. And there are things we can do to get better sleep.

Regular exercise has been proven to improve sleep quality and reduce insomnia symptoms. Engaging in moderate-intensity exercises, such as walking, yoga, or swimming, can promote better sleep and overall well-being.

I know I keep bringing it up, but it actually does work.

However, it's essential to avoid strenuous exercise close to bedtime, as it can increase alertness and make it harder to fall asleep.

Menopause can have an impact on so many levels, as earlier mentioned. Such as sexual health, insomnia or disrupted sleep patterns, which can lead to fatigue and irritability. Physical activity promotes the release of serotonin, a neurotransmitter that regulates sleep mood and gets the juices pumping.

Exercise helps combat the physical changes that occur during menopause.

Regular physical activity can prevent weight gain and reduce the risk of developing chronic conditions such as heart disease, diabetes, and osteoporosis. Weight-bearing exercises, such as walking, jogging, or weightlifting, can also help maintain bone density and reduce the risk of osteoporosis-related fractures. Estrogen plays a crucial role in maintaining healthy bones and joints, and its decline can lead to increased inflammation and reduced lubrication in the joints.

This can result in feelings of discomfort, stiffness, and reduced flexibility. We miss our estrogen, don't we?

Remember to consult with your healthcare provider before starting any exercise regimen and choose activities that you like making this journey a more enjoyable and empowering one.

Cardiovascular Exercise: Engaging in aerobic activities like walking, swimming, cycling, or dancing helps strengthen the heart and lungs while boosting mood and energy levels. Dancing in your living room while singing your favorite song counts and it feels great. Or go out dancing and get your cardio done at the same time.

Strength Training: Menopause is often accompanied by a decline in muscle mass and bone density. Incorporating strength training exercises such as weightlifting, resistance band workouts, or bodyweight exercises can help build and maintain muscle strength, improve posture, and reduce the risk of osteoporosis.

Remember, weights can be just water bottles filled with water; you don't have to join a gym or buy expensive equipment.

Incorporate these exercises into your daily routine for optimal results. I know the list is long, but remember, just a little bit is so much better than nothing. Find the things that are easy for you to do, and eventually add more. And again, celebrate every little progress you discover.

Mindfulness and Meditation: Can greatly benefit you by helping reduce stress, anxiety, and depression often experienced during menopause. Regular mindfulness exercises, deep breathing, or guided meditation can promote better mental health and improve sleep quality. Just being in the moment while you take a walk or enjoying a sunset can give you a small brain time out.

Yoga and Pilates: These mind-body exercises can be particularly beneficial. Yoga helps improve flexibility, balance, and strength while also reducing stress and promoting relaxation. Pilates focuses on core strength, stability, and flexibility, aiding in better posture and alleviating back pain. Both practices can also enhance mental well-being and promote better sleep. Again, you don't have to join a class if that isn't possible for you.

There are several free videos online; just make room on the floor and try it out.

I mainly do strength and cardio, but realized my flexibility was not what it used to be.

So, I've joined a yoga class, and let's just say there is a lot of groaning and puffing, even the occasional fart. But we laugh it off and reassure each other that we are all in there trying our best to feel better.

My notes

Chapter 5
Managing Symptoms Naturally

We know by now that hormonal imbalance is a big challenge in menopause. Fluctuating estrogen and progesterone levels can lead to a variety of symptoms. Nature can lend a helping hand.

It's important to also limit the consumption of saturated and trans fats typically found in fried and processed foods, as they can negatively affect heart health. Instead, incorporating heart-healthy fats such as those found in avocados, nuts, and olive oil can contribute positively to cholesterol levels.

Some menopausal symptoms can be alleviated by consuming phytoestrogen-rich foods like soy, flaxseeds, and legumes, which mimic the effects of estrogen in the body.

Joint pain and muscle stiffness: can be managed by adopting an anti-inflammatory diet. Including foods rich in omega-3 fatty acids, such as fatty fish, walnuts, and flaxseeds, can help reduce inflammation.

Overall joint health: can be supported by consuming a variety of fruits, vegetables, whole grains, and lean proteins, providing essential nutrients.

Bone loss: can be countered by including calcium-rich foods such as dairy products, leafy greens, and fortified plant-based milk.

Brain health and mood can be improved by consuming a diet rich in omega-3 fatty acids, found in fatty fish like salmon, walnuts, and chia seeds. Additionally, cognitive function can be enhanced and the risk of mental health issues reduced by incorporating B vitamins from whole grains, leafy greens, and lean proteins.

Improve sexual function and desire by including foods like oysters, dark chocolate, and avocado, which are rich in zinc, magnesium, and healthy fats, can enhance blood flow, promote hormone production, and increase libido.

Sleep disturbances can be helped by avoiding caffeine and alcohol close to bedtime and consuming sleep-promoting foods like cherries, bananas, and whole grains can help regulate sleep patterns and improve the quality of sleep.

Incorporating a diet rich in fruits, vegetables, whole grains, and lean proteins can provide the necessary fuel for exercise and support optimal health.

You can also consult with a healthcare professional or nutritionist to create a personalized dietary plan that meets individual needs and preferences.

Herbal Remedies and Supplements

Fortunately, there are various herbal remedies and supplements available that can help alleviate some symptoms and promote overall well-being. Let's explore some of the most popular and effective options that we may consider. But remember to always take this up with your healthcare professional before use.

Hot flashes, night sweats, and mood swings may be reduced by herbal supplements like black cohosh, dong quai, and red clover. With compounds mimicking estrogen, they can offer relief by restoring hormonal balance.

Mental Health: To address these issues, herbal remedies like St. John's Wort and evening primrose oil have shown promise in reducing symptoms of depression and promoting a positive mood. Additionally, omega-3 fatty acids found in fish oil can support brain health and cognitive function.

Sleep Issues: Herbal remedies such as valerian root, chamomile, and lavender can promote relaxation and improve sleep quality. Melatonin supplements can also be beneficial in regulating sleep patterns and promoting a restful night's sleep.

Sexual Health: Herbal supplements like black cohosh and ginseng can help boost libido and improve sexual function. Additionally, maca root has been used for centuries to enhance sexual desire and alleviate symptoms of low libido.

Exercise: Herbal remedies like ginkgo biloba can help improve memory and concentration, making it easier to engage in physical activities. Additionally, supplements like magnesium can reduce muscle cramps and promote better exercise performance.

It is important to note that while herbal remedies and supplements can be effective, it is always recommended to consult with a healthcare professional before starting any new regimen, especially if you have existing medical conditions or are taking prescription medications.

My notes

_____

_____

_____

_____

_____

_____

_____

_____

_____

_____

_____

_____

_____

_____

_____

_____

_____

_____

_____

_____

_____

_____

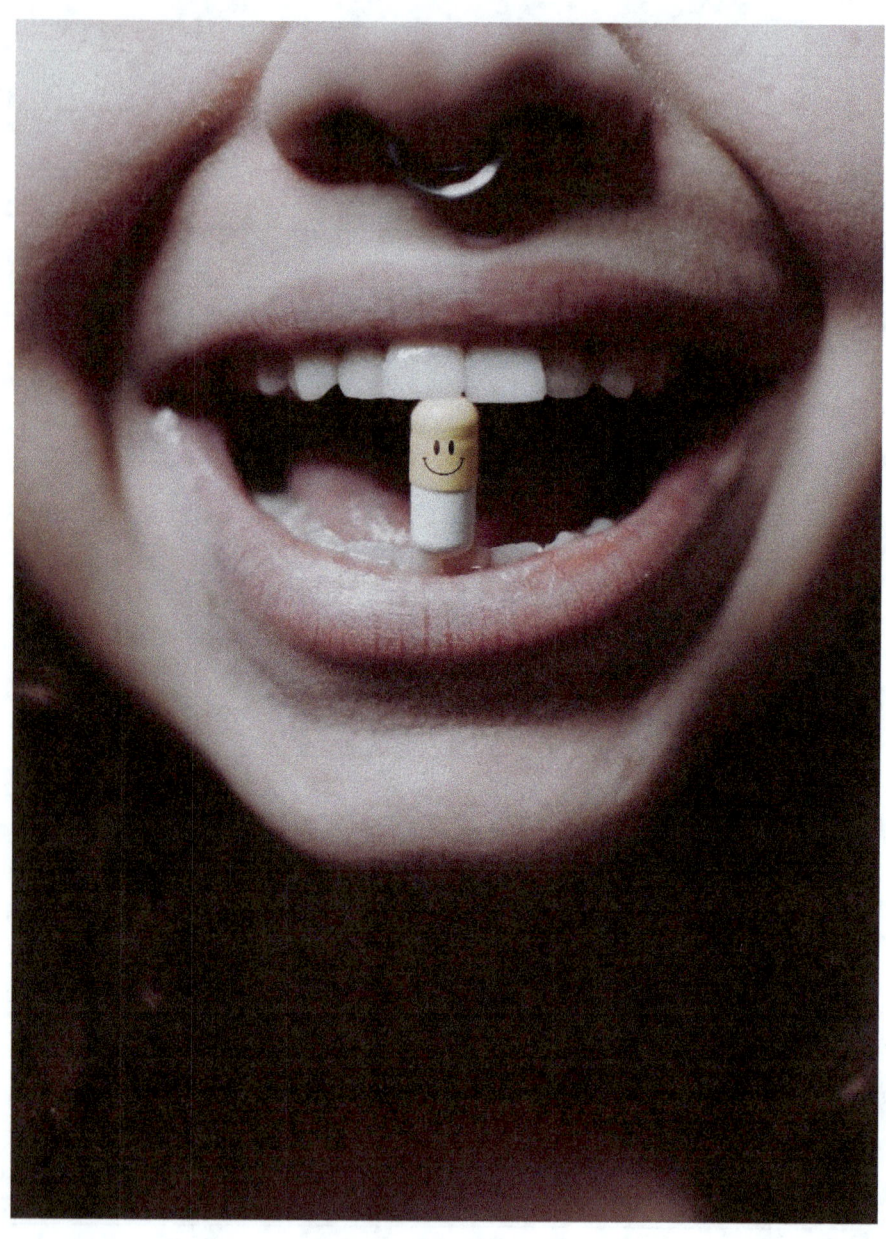

CHAPTER 6
HORMONE REPLACEMENT THERAPY (HRT)

Understanding HRT and its Benefits and Risks

Hormone Replacement Therapy (HRT) can be prescribed treatment for women going through menopause. It involves the use of medications that contain female hormones, such as estrogen and progesterone, to replace those that the body no longer produces in sufficient amounts. HRT can, for some, be very beneficial in managing the various symptoms associated with menopause, such as:

Hot flashes, night sweats, and vaginal dryness. HRT can effectively reduce the frequency and severity of these symptoms, providing much-needed relief.

Additionally, HRT can help maintain bone density, reducing the risk of osteoporosis, a condition that becomes more prevalent after menopause.

Many experience mood swings, irritability, anxiety, and even depression during menopause. The fluctuation of hormones can have a significant impact on emotional well-being. HRT might help stabilize hormone levels, leading to improved mental health and overall emotional stability.

By restoring hormonal balance, HRT can enhance sexual desire, increase vaginal lubrication, and alleviate any discomfort, allowing you to maintain a healthy and fulfilling sex life.

Night sweats and insomnia can disrupt sleep patterns, leading to fatigue and reduced quality of life. HRT can help regulate hormones and alleviate these sleep disturbances, promoting better sleep and improved overall energy levels.

However, it is important to note that HRT is not suitable for everyone. Individual medical history, risk factors, and personal preferences should be taken into consideration when discussing HRT with a healthcare provider. It is essential to have a thorough understanding of the benefits, potential risks, and alternatives before deciding.

It is crucial for us to understand the potential risks and side effects associated with HRT to make informed decisions about our health.

One of the primary concerns with HRT is an increased risk of certain health conditions. Research has shown that long-term use of estrogen and progestin, the hormones used in combination HRT, may slightly elevate the risk of breast cancer. Regular mammograms and self-examinations are recommended for women on HRT.

Additionally, HRT may slightly increase the risk of developing blood clots or stroke. This risk is particularly relevant for women who are overweight, smoke or have a history of cardiovascular disease. It is crucial to discuss these potential risks with your healthcare provider and weigh them against the benefits of HRT in managing your menopause symptoms.

Apart from these risks, some women may experience side effects when starting HRT. These side effects can include breast tenderness, bloating, mood swings, and headaches. However, these symptoms typically subside as the body adjusts to the hormonal changes. If side effects persist or become severe, it is essential to consult your healthcare provider for alternative treatment options.

Furthermore, women should be aware that HRT may not be suitable for everyone. Those with a history of certain cancers, liver disease, or blood clotting disorders may be advised against HRT. Your healthcare provider will assess your medical history and individual circumstances to determine the most appropriate treatment plan for you.

Different Types of HRT

Estrogen Therapy: Estrogen therapy, the most common form of HRT, focuses on replenishing the declining levels of estrogen. This treatment can be delivered through various methods, such as pills, patches, creams, or vaginal rings. Estrogen therapy effectively addresses symptoms like hot flashes, vaginal dryness, and night sweats.

Combination Therapy: Combination therapy combines estrogen with progestin, a synthetic form of progesterone. This type of HRT is typically recommended for women who still have their uterus. Progestin helps protect the uterus from developing endometrial cancer, which can occur when estrogen is taken alone. Combination therapy is available in various forms, including pills, patches, and creams.

Bioidentical Hormone Therapy: Bioidentical hormones are derived from plant sources and are designed to closely mimic the natural hormones found in a woman's body. These hormones, available in creams, gels, or pellets, are customized based on individual needs.

Bioidentical hormone therapy may provide relief from menopause symptoms and is believed to have fewer side effects than traditional HRT.

However, more research is required to fully understand the benefits and risks.

Low-Dose HRT: Low-dose HRT involves using the smallest effective amount of hormones to manage menopause symptoms. This approach aims to minimize potential risks associated with long-term hormone use. Low-dose HRT is often recommended for women who experience mild to moderate symptoms or are concerned about the side effects of higher doses.

Localized HRT: Localized HRT focuses on delivering hormones directly to the affected area, such as the vagina, to alleviate symptoms like vaginal dryness or discomfort during intercourse.

This method typically involves using creams, rings, or tablets that release hormones locally.

It is crucial to remember that every woman's experience with menopause is unique. Therefore, finding the right type of HRT requires open communication with your healthcare provider. Together, you can assess your individual symptoms, medical history, and personal preferences to determine the most suitable HRT approach for you.

By navigating the various options available, you can improve your menopause journey, ensuring a smoother transition and enhanced overall well-being.

My notes

_____

_____

_____

_____

_____

_____

_____

_____

_____

_____

_____

_____

_____

_____

_____

_____

_____

_____

_____

_____

_____

CHAPTER 7
MAINTAINING BONE HEALTH

Understanding Bone Loss and Osteoporosis

As we enter menopause, other common concerns enter our lives, namely Bone loss and the development of osteoporosis. It is crucial for us to understand the implications of bone loss and take proactive steps to maintain our bone health.

During menopause, the body experiences a decline in estrogen levels, which plays a crucial role in maintaining bone strength. This decrease in estrogen can lead to accelerated bone loss and increase the risk of osteoporosis, a condition characterized by weak and brittle bones. Osteoporosis can make us more susceptible to fractures, particularly in the spine, hips, and wrists, and significantly impact our quality of life.

To combat bone loss and reduce the risk of osteoporosis, we need to focus on adopting a bone-healthy lifestyle. This includes ensuring an adequate intake of calcium and vitamin D through a balanced diet or supplements.

Calcium-rich foods such as dairy products, leafy greens, and fortified cereals can provide a good foundation, while exposure to sunlight or vitamin D supplements can help the body absorb and utilize calcium effectively.

In addition to bone health, calcium and vitamin D also play a crucial role in supporting mental health. Studies have shown that women with low levels of these nutrients are more susceptible to depression and anxiety during menopause. Ensuring adequate intake of calcium and vitamin D can help alleviate these symptoms and improve overall mental well-being. That's a win-win

Lastly, maintaining optimal calcium and vitamin D levels is essential for women in menopause who wish to engage in regular exercise. These nutrients support muscle function and strength, reducing the risk of falls and injuries during physical activity.

Regular exercise is also paramount for maintaining bone health during menopause. Weight-bearing exercises, such as walking, jogging, dancing, or weightlifting, stimulate the bones to become stronger and denser. Additionally, strength training exercises can help improve balance and reduce the risk of falls, which can be particularly detrimental for women with weakened bones.

Weight-bearing exercises involve working against gravity while staying on your feet and include activities like walking, hiking, dancing, and stair climbing. These exercises stimulate the bones, promoting the formation of new bone tissue and improving overall bone strength. They also provide numerous additional benefits, such as improving balance, coordination, and muscle strength.

Walking is a fantastic weight-bearing exercise accessible to almost everyone. Whether you prefer a leisurely stroll in the park or a brisk power walk, it can be easily integrated into your daily routine. Aim for at least 30 minutes of walking most days of the week. Additionally, consider adding some hills or inclines to challenge your muscles and bones further.

Dancing is another enjoyable weight-bearing activity that offers both physical and mental health benefits. Whether it's ballroom dancing, belly dancing, or just livingroom dancing, moving to music can help increase bone density while promoting social connections and boosting your mood.

Stair climbing is an excellent way to incorporate weight-bearing exercise into your daily life. Instead of taking the elevator or escalator, opt for the stairs whenever possible. This simple change can make a significant difference in strengthening your bones and improving cardiovascular health.

If you prefer a more structured exercise routine, consider joining a strength training class or working with a personal trainer. Incorporating exercises using resistance bands or free weights can help build muscle strength, which in turn supports and protects your bones.

Remember, it's essential to consult with your healthcare provider before starting any new exercise program, especially if you have any pre-existing medical conditions or concerns. They can help you determine which exercises are most suitable for your specific needs.

Take charge of your bone health during menopause and enjoy the many additional benefits that come with regular exercise.

Bone Density Tests and Medications

Bone density tests, also known as DXA scans, are non-invasive procedures that measure the density of your bones. These tests provide critical information about your bone health and can help identify the risk of fractures or osteoporosis.

They allow healthcare professionals to assess your bone strength and determine the need for preventive measures or medications.

If you are experiencing menopause-related bone loss, your healthcare provider may recommend medication to help maintain bone density and reduce the risk of fractures. The most common medications prescribed for this purpose are bisphosphonates, selective estrogen receptor modulators (SERMs), and hormone therapy (HT).

Bisphosphonates work by slowing down the breakdown of bones, thereby increasing bone density. They are typically taken orally or via injection and have been shown to reduce the risk of fractures. However, it's important to discuss the potential side effects and benefits of bisphosphonates with your doctor before starting this treatment.

SERMs, such as raloxifene, mimic estrogen's effects on bones and help preserve bone density. These medications can also reduce the risk of breast cancer. However, like any medication, SERMs come with potential side effects, including hot flashes and blood clots. Your healthcare provider will help you weigh the risks and benefits to determine if SERMs are suitable for you.

Hormone Replacement Therapy (HRT), which involves estrogen and progesterone supplementation, can also be prescribed to manage bone loss during menopause. HRT not only helps maintain bone density but also relieves other menopause symptoms like hot flashes and vaginal dryness. However, HRT may increase the risk of certain health conditions, such as blood clots and breast cancer.

Therefore, it is crucial to discuss your medical history with your doctor to determine if HRT is a safe option for you.

However, it is essential to have an open and honest discussion with your healthcare provider to understand the benefits and potential risks associated with these medications.

My notes

_____

_____

_____

_____

_____

_____

_____

_____

_____

_____

_____

_____

_____

_____

_____

_____

_____

_____

_____

_____

CHAPTER 8
TAKING CARE OF YOUR HEART

While discussions about hot flashes, mood swings, and sleep disturbances are common, the impact of menopause on heart health often receives less attention.

However, it's imperative for us to recognize the potential risks and take necessary measures to safeguard our cardiovascular well-being. Significant hormonal shifts occurring within our bodies during menopause can affect cholesterol levels and blood pressure, potentially elevating the risk of cardiovascular diseases.

Estrogen, essential for maintaining healthy blood vessels, declines during menopause, leading to changes in cholesterol metabolism.

Additionally, menopause can contribute to increased blood pressure levels due to reduced flexibility and function of blood vessels. Being mindful of these changes and taking proactive steps to mitigate potential health risks is crucial during menopause. In some cases, lifestyle adjustments alone may not suffice to control cholesterol and blood pressure, prompting healthcare professionals to recommend medication for effective management.

Regular check-ups and open discussions with healthcare providers are essential during menopause to monitor and address any emerging health concerns.
It's important to acknowledge that women are also susceptible to cardiovascular diseases during menopause, contrary to the misconception that it primarily affects men.

Research indicates that menopause can heighten the risk of heart disease due to the decline in estrogen, which plays a protective role in maintaining healthy blood vessels and reducing inflammation.

As estrogen levels decrease, adverse changes in lipid profiles, including elevated LDL cholesterol and decreased HDL cholesterol, may occur, contributing to arterial plaque buildup and increased heart disease risk. Furthermore, menopause often coincides with other heart disease risk factors such as weight gain, elevated blood pressure, and insulin resistance, exacerbating the cardiovascular risk.

Adopting a heart-healthy lifestyle is essential to minimize the risk of heart disease during menopause.

I know, I know - more gloom and doom, but knowing is empowering you -take care.

Regular exercise, including aerobic activities like brisk walking, swimming, or cycling for at least 150 minutes per week, can significantly improve heart health, reduce blood pressure, and help manage weight.

Maintaining a balanced, nutritious diet centered around whole foods while limiting processed foods, sugary beverages, and high-sodium meals is equally crucial.

Additionally, quitting smoking and moderating alcohol intake are vital steps in reducing heart disease risk. Regular check-ups with healthcare providers are crucial for monitoring heart health during menopause, including discussions about individual risk factors and appropriate screening tests such as cholesterol and blood pressure measurements to detect potential issues early.

Remember, taking care of your heart is a vital part of the journey through menopause and beyond.

Consuming a diverse range of nutrient-rich foods plays a crucial role in weight management, as well as in controlling cholesterol levels and blood pressure, ultimately lowering the risk of heart diseases.

A balanced diet that includes an abundance of fruits, vegetables, whole grains, and lean proteins is key to achieving these health goals.

Your healthcare provider may also recommend additional tests, such as an electrocardiogram (ECG) or stress test, to evaluate the heart's function and detect any abnormalities.

In addition to regular check-ups, it is crucial to be aware of the symptoms of cardiovascular diseases:

- *Shortness of breath or difficulty breathing
- *A tightening sensation in the chest, as if the bra is too tight
- *Pain in the diaphragm and stomach and pain radiates to the back or up to the jaw
- *Nausea and vomiting
- *Feeling of palpitations
- *Dizziness and fainting
- *General discomfort
- *Discomfort and faintness

If you experience any of these symptoms, it is important to seek medical attention promptly.

My notes

CHAPTER 9
MENTAL HEALTH

The dreaded change

Menopause can trigger a range of emotions, including mood swings, irritability, anxiety, and even depression. These emotional changes can be attributed to the hormonal fluctuations that occur as the ovaries gradually cease hormone production. Estrogen, in particular, plays a crucial role in regulating mood, and its decline can lead to emotional rollercoaster rides. Yes estrogen again, the source of so much fun and lack of the same.

I was talking to one of my closest friends, and she said: "Some mornings, I wake up feeling fragile, and I just know it's going to be a day where I need to be my own best friend. "Now that is great advise. Note to self, on hard days, be extra kind to yourself, like you would be to a friend or family member. "Other days, I wake up feeling so done with everyone and everything, and I know I need to take a lot of deep breaths to avoid killing anyone.". I know that feeling, too.

Don´t get me wrong, my BS filter also definitely got firmer. I reached an age where I find myself thinking, "I am too old for this s..." Sometimes, that means I set a boundary, and other times, I realize that someone or something just isn´t important enough to me to get involved anymore. And that is actually a relief. But the mood swings are tough.

You may find yourself feeling more easily irritated or frustrated and may have difficulty managing stress. It is important to recognize that these emotional changes are a normal part of the menopause journey and that you are not alone in experiencing them.

Talking to friends and family or joining support groups specifically for women in menopause can provide a safe space to share experiences and gain valuable insights.

Addressing mental health during menopause is equally important. Many women experience increased anxiety or feelings of sadness. Some may even develop symptoms of depression, which further impacts overall quality of life. Seeking professional help from a therapist or counselor who specializes in menopause and mental health can provide effective strategies for coping with these emotional changes.

Decreased libido and changes in sexual satisfaction are common concerns that can affect self-esteem and intimate relationships. Open communication with your partner and healthcare provider can really help you find solutions.

If your partner is going through menopause, too, they might very well be dealing with all this as well. Regardless of your partner's gender!

It's not a topic often talked about, but men actually go through many of the same and some different changes. (That might be a topic for another book)

Sleep disturbances often accompany menopause, and these can further exacerbate emotional changes. Many of us have trouble falling asleep, staying asleep, or wake up feeling unrefreshed. Practicing good sleep hygiene, such as creating a relaxing bedtime routine and maintaining a cool, dark, and quiet sleep environment, can aid in improving sleep quality. (chapter 3 may be helpful)

If sleep issues persist, consult with a healthcare professional who can recommend appropriate interventions.

Managing Mood Swings

Let's be honest. Mood swings suck at any age; it can be overwhelming and isolating. Understanding that you are not alone in this journey is empowering. and with some strategies and support, it is possible to alleviate and manage mood swings to some degree.

Seeking emotional support is vital when experiencing mood swings. Connecting with friends and family or joining support groups can provide a safe space for sharing experiences and finding solace. Moreover, professional help, such as therapy or counseling, can equip us with coping strategies and tools to manage mood swings effectively. Find your coven, team, people whatever you want to call them.

Managing mood swings requires a multifaceted approach. Prioritize your mental and emotional well-being by adopting a healthy lifestyle, establishing proper sleep hygiene, seeking emotional support, and addressing sexual health concerns. It is essential to remember that menopause is a transformative phase. This, too, shall pass!

One effective coping strategy for managing anxiety and depression during menopause is seeking professional help. Consulting with a healthcare provider, such as a gynecologist or a mental health professional, can provide valuable guidance tailored to individual needs. They may recommend various treatment options, including hormone therapy, antidepressant medications, or therapy techniques such as cognitive-behavioral therapy (CBT).

In addition to professional help, there are several self-care practices that you can incorporate into your daily life to alleviate symptoms. Regular exercise has been proven to reduce anxiety and depression. Engaging in activities such as yoga, swimming, or walking not only helps release endorphins but also promotes overall well-being.

Maintaining a healthy sleep routine is also crucial for managing mental health during menopause. Sleep disturbances are a common symptom, and poor sleep can exacerbate anxiety and depression. Creating a relaxing bedtime routine, practicing good sleep hygiene, and making the bedroom a sleep-friendly environment can significantly improve sleep quality.

Pimp your space! Make your bedroom an oasis for you to relax in; little things might be all it takes. Get rid of stuff in there that doesn't belong there or things that annoy you.

If that thing is your partner, take deep breaths and think it through. You might want to keep them. My husband is a big-time snorer. With my own problems sleeping, his snoring felt like he was showing off. I tried sleeping in another room, but that doesn't work for us. And not everyone has that option. So, in my case sound cancelling earbuds did the trick.

After trying different types, I finally found some that are both soft and comfortable and give me complete silence. Gamechanger for me.

My sleep has improved immensely and with that, my mood and energy to do stuff.

Finally, it's essential for everyone to engage in activities that bring them joy and relaxation. Pursuing hobbies, spending time with loved ones, and practicing mindfulness or meditation techniques can provide a sense of balance and reduce stress levels. Whatever rocks your boat -do it. It might even be something you haven't done in years. Think back to what made you happy earlier on.

Many of us haven't had time to think about what we want for such a long time, taking care of work, family, and daily life. Maybe now is the perfect time to think about what you really like and want.

Stress Reduction Techniques

As we navigate this transition, it is essential to prioritize self-care and find effective ways to manage stress. Stress reduction techniques can play a significant role in promoting overall well-being.

<u>Mindfulness and Meditation</u>: Practicing mindfulness and meditation techniques can help cultivate a sense of calm and reduce stress. Mindfulness involves being fully present in the moment, without judgment, and paying attention to your thoughts, feelings, and bodily sensations.
I have had a strong meditation routine for many years but experienced a new difficulty focusing while my husband was sick.

This was extremely frustrating and after struggling for some time, I simply decided to start all over learning the well-known techniques all over again. And that turned out to be a very effective strategy for me.

I regained my confidence and started enjoying my practice again. Be very patient with yourself; just 2 minutes of focus is a win. If you want to, you can get there. Some days, I still struggle, but it is okay.

<u>Deep Breathing Exercises:</u> Deep breathing is a simple yet powerful technique that can be practiced anywhere, anytime. By taking slow, deep breaths, you can activate your body's relaxation response, decrease stress levels, and promote a sense of tranquility. There are so many great apps and exercises online. Find one that you feel comfortable with.

<u>Yoga and Tai Chi:</u> Engaging in gentle exercises like yoga and tai chi can be highly beneficial going

through menopause. These practices not only provide physical benefits but also help manage stress, improve flexibility, and promote mental clarity.

Communication and Support: Connecting with others who are experiencing similar challenges can provide immense emotional support. Joining menopause support groups or seeking therapy can create a safe space for you to share your concerns, gain valuable insights, and reduce stress.

Prioritizing Sleep Hygiene: Quality sleep is crucial for managing stress and promoting overall health. Establishing a regular sleep routine, creating a comfortable sleep environment, and practicing relaxation techniques before bedtime can significantly improve sleep quality. (Yes, it is that important!)

Regular Exercise: Engaging in regular physical activity has numerous benefits for everyone. Exercise not only helps maintain weight and bone density but also releases endorphins, which are natural mood boosters and stress reducers.

Self-Care Practices: Incorporating self-care activities into daily routines can significantly reduce stress levels. Taking time for yourself, indulging in hobbies, practicing gratitude, and engaging in activities that bring joy and relaxation can help.

Taking time for yourself might feel like an impossible task, but remember, like the oxygen mask on the plane, you need to take care of yourself to be able to be there for anyone else.

By implementing these stress reduction techniques, we can enhance our mental well-being, improve sexual health, promote better sleep, and maintain an active life. It is crucial to remember that everyone's experience is unique, and finding the right combination of strategies may require some exploration.

My notes

CHAPTER 10
NAVIGATING LIFE

One of the most common challenges faced by women in the workplace is managing menopause-related hot flashes. These sudden waves of heat can be embarrassing and uncomfortable, but there are ways to alleviate their impact. Dressing in layers, choosing materials that are breathable, keeping a small fan at your desk, and staying hydrated can help regulate body temperature and minimize the disruption caused by hot flashes.

I always have a fan in my bag, and I'm not too shy to use it.

To some, it might look strange, but I embrace the wisdom of the women from southern Europe who use this so much.

I have wondered where to put this next part, but it is so important to me, and I feel it needs to be mentioned. The idea that we should no longer dress as we like because of age frustrates me.

That we, especially as women, try to tell each other how to dress, what our hair should look like and what makeup and accessories are appropriate. The choice must be YOURS! If you feel like having long red hair, go for it, and if you feel best in all beige, you do you.

As long as you're not harming anyone else or breaking real laws. I will not let anyone stop me from wearing colorful, sometimes wild and fun clothes.

Getting older is a privilege not everyone gets to experience, so let's celebrate it in every possible way.

Including the way, we present our personality and our choices to the world.

Don't get me wrong, I'm not without fault; sometimes I do catch myself thinking, "Wau, how does she even keep her eyes open with those lashes?". But I try to stop, and I try to give compliments whenever I see someone who inspires me or just looks great.

No one ever got offended and to be honest, I love getting compliments myself. And I'm getting better at accepting them, too.

My grandma used to say If you have nothing positive to say don't say anything – I will add, and if you do, please share it.

We need more sunshine in our world.

When it comes to communicating with employers about menopause, it is essential to remember that they may not be fully aware of the impact it can have on your well-being and productivity. Start by educating yourself about your rights and the resources available to support you during this period. Familiarize yourself with any policies or guidelines that may be in place to address menopause-related issues. This knowledge will empower you to have informed discussions with your employer.

Colleagues can play a crucial role in creating a supportive work environment during menopause. However, it is up to you to decide how much you want to disclose about your personal experience. If you feel comfortable sharing, consider discussing your menopause journey with trusted colleagues.

This can help them understand any changes in your behavior or performance and foster empathy and support. They might very well be facing the same difficulties. Wouldn't it be wonderful if menopause was no longer a taboo, but a topic to be talked about openly.

Remember, effective communication is crucial for maintaining your well-being and productivity. By educating yourself, initiating open conversations, and seeking support when needed, you can create a more understanding and supportive work environment. Together, we can navigate menopause with confidence and empower ourselves to thrive both personally and professionally.

Employers should prioritize mental health support and, if possible, provide resources such as counseling services or access to mental health professionals. Creating awareness about the impact of menopause on mental health can help reduce stigma and foster a more inclusive workplace.

Sleep issues often accompany menopause, leading to fatigue and decreased productivity. Employers can promote better sleep hygiene by encouraging regular breaks, creating designated rest areas, or providing flexible working hours when possible. Implementing policies that prioritize employee well-being, such as limiting late-night work demands or promoting relaxation techniques, can significantly contribute to improved sleep quality.

Lastly, regular exercise has been shown to alleviate menopausal symptoms and improve overall health. Employers should support physical activity by offering gym memberships, organizing exercises during work hours, or encouraging walking meetings. Promoting movement and exercise not only benefits women in menopause but also enhances team-building and fosters a positive work culture.

Embrace the Next Chapter of Life

This marks a transition into a new phase of life, and it is crucial to acknowledge the personal growth and wisdom you have gained along the way. Reflect on the challenges you have overcome, the lessons you have learned, and the strength you have developed. Recognizing your growth, you are older and wiser - and that is not bad at all!

So your boobs no longer salute the world; well, maybe it's time you salute yourself.

My notes

_____
_____
_____
_____
_____
_____
_____
_____
_____
_____
_____
_____
_____
_____
_____
_____
_____
_____
_____
_____

Sources that provide more information

1. PubMed: PubMed is a free search engine accessing primarily the MEDLINE database of references and abstracts on life sciences and biomedical topics. It contains numerous studies on the effects of diet, hydration, and herbal supplements.
2. National Institutes of Health (NIH): The NIH provides comprehensive information on women's health.
3. Mayo Clinic: Mayo Clinic's website offers reliable information on various health topics, including vaginal dryness and natural remedies. Their articles are written and reviewed by medical professionals.
4. WebMD: WebMD is a reputable source for health information featuring articles, expert opinions, and research findings on vaginal dryness and alternative treatments.
5. Academic Journals: Journals such as the "Journal of Women's Health," "Menopause," and "The Journal of Sexual Medicine" often publish research articles on topics related to vaginal health and natural remedies.

6. Books: There are several books written by healthcare professionals specializing in women's health. Examples include "The V Book: A Doctor's Guide to Complete Vulvovaginal Health" by Elizabeth G. Stewart and "The Hormone Cure" by Sara Gottfried.
7. Women's Health Organizations: Websites of organizations like the American College of Obstetricians and Gynecologists (ACOG) or the North American Menopause Society (NAMS) often provide information and resources on women's health issues.

www.ingramcontent.com/pod-product-compliance
Lightning Source LLC
Chambersburg PA
CBHW071019120626
46546CB00003B/1155